STATIONS OF THE CROSS

FOR TEENAGERS

Gwen Costello

GW00567525

TWENTY-THIRD PUBLICATIONS
Mystic, Connecticut

Ninth printing 1995

Twenty-Third Publications
185 Willow Street
P.O. Box 180
Mystic CT 06355
(203) 536-2611
800-321-0411

ISBN 0-89622-386-8

All illustrations, including cover, are computer-enhanced
photos of the stations of the cross in St. Matthew Cathedral
in Washington, D.C.

Before You Begin…

> "If anyone wants to come with me, he or she must put aside self-interest, and then pick up the cross and follow me. Pursuing self-interest leads to nothing in the end, but putting aside self-interest for my sake leads to everything."
>
> Matthew 16:24 (adapted)

Jesus spoke these words to his first followers. And now he is speaking them to you. Yes, you. Though "only a teenager," you are a person of great worth in Jesus' eyes, so great that he is inviting you to follow him.

And how might you follow Jesus? First of all by putting aside your own selfish interests. This requires looking around you at other people whose wants and needs are more important than your own. By caring for others and taking responsibility for them you are picking up the cross to follow Jesus.

In the following pages, walk the Stations of the Cross with Jesus. Open your mind and heart and allow him to speak to you, to teach you. In doing so you will lose nothing. Indeed, you will gain everything.

First Station

Jesus Is Condemned

Every day in our world people are condemned. We hear about it on the evening news. Every time someone is rejected for being black or Asian, Hispanic or Jewish, every time an old person has to huddle on a street corner to keep warm or search in a garbage can for food, every time a handicapped person is made to feel unwelcome, someone is being condemned. You see it at school too. There are kids who are constantly the butt of jokes. They look funny or talk funny, and they don't know how to dress. They just don't fit in.

Jesus was one of those who didn't fit in. He did and said things that upset the people with the power. The religious leaders wanted him out of the way and Pilate the judge went along with them. Jesus was condemned to die on a cross.

(Pause for silent reflection.)

Jesus, forgive us for the times we have condemned you in others through our silence and indifference. Help us to love and welcome all others as you did. Teach us how to follow you.

Second Station

Jesus Carries the Cross

All around us people are carrying heavy burdens.
Some of these burdens we know about, like the
ones our parents carry. But we ignore them. Some
burdens we don't know about, like the ones carried
by teachers or other kids in our classes. But we don't
really care. Others we hear about on the news, like
war, hunger, poverty, and injustice. But we can't be
bothered with what goes on elsewhere in the world.
We allow ourselves to be deaf and blind to the pain
of others. It's easier that way. We have enough to
do just taking care of ourselves.

Jesus was forced to carry the burden of the cross.
Surely there were those in the crowd who knew
him. They saw the soldiers drop the cross on his
shoulders, but they were worried about themselves.
They didn't protest the rough treatment he received;
they didn't come forward.

(Pause for silent reflection.)

Jesus, forgive us for the times we have walked
away from the burdens of others. Help us not to be
deaf and blind to their pain. Teach us how to follow
you.

Third Station

Jesus Falls the First Time

The worst thing that can happen to us is to fall flat on our faces in front of others: when we do or say something stupid, when we're not accepted for who we are, when we're laughed at for not looking right or dressing right. To be shut out is the worst way to fall flat. At school games or dances, we know there are kids who are on the outside looking in. But we don't invite them in. What would our friends think?

Jesus fell flat in front of the soldiers, in front of people who had believed in him, in front of his own mother. He was in this situation because he had spoken out and taken risks for others. Look where it got him. What must he have been thinking as he lost control and fell under the cross?

(Pause for silent reflection.)

Jesus, forgive us for the times we have shut others out and refused to help. Help us to be aware of their needs. Teach us how to follow you.

Fourth Station

Jesus Meets His Mother

Parents expect so much of us. They want us to succeed. They want to believe that we can get good grades, that everyone will like us, that we will never cheat or lie or steal, that we will always choose what is right. And we want our parents to think the best of us; we don't want them to know about some of the things we do.

Mary wanted Jesus to succeed. She wanted people to accept him, to believe him, to love him. But here she meets him and he is carrying a criminal's cross. Did she think that he was guilty, that he was a failure? Or did she love and support him?

(Pause for silent reflection.)

Jesus, forgive us for the times we have resented our parents. Help us to be grateful for their love and support. Teach us how to follow you.

Fifth Station

Simon Helps Jesus

Sometimes a teacher makes us sit next to an "outsider," or makes us help someone we wouldn't be caught dead with. We don't stop to think about that other person's feelings. We only care about how we feel. How does this look to our friends? What if they think we chose this situation?

Poor Simon. Why was he, a foreigner, chosen to help this "criminal" carry his cross? Would people think he was a criminal too? He was probably embarrassed and humiliated to be forced into this situation. Was there even a moment when he forgot his own discomfort and looked with compassion at Jesus?

(Pause for silent reflection.)

Jesus, forgive us for the times we have hurt others by not caring how they feel. Show us how to act with love and compassion. Teach us how to follow you.

Sixth Station

Veronica Wipes Jesus' Face

There are people who sometimes actually buck the crowd. When everyone else is drinking, or doing drugs, or telling crude jokes, or tearing someone down, this person speaks up. "Hey, this isn't right; this isn't good. I refuse to go along." And everyone laughs.

Veronica bucked the crowd. Her sympathy overcame her fear, and she came forward to wipe the blood and sweat from Jesus' face. She didn't stop to think about the consequences or to measure her own needs. At that moment she thought only about the needs of Jesus.

(Pause for silent reflection.)

Jesus, forgive us for the times we have laughed at people who bucked the crowd. Help us learn to accept the truth about ourselves and the things we do. Teach us how to follow you.

Seventh Station

Jesus Falls Again

Failure is a terrible thing. None of us wants to be a failure, especially in the eyes of our friends. Parents and teachers might think of us as failures, but when friends do, it's too much. All day we are concerned about what our friends will think, and we work hard to look good in their eyes. But sometimes they fail us. They don't stand by us when we need them, in spite of all our efforts to please them.

When Jesus fell again, what were his concerns? Was he worried about how his friends were taking this? And where were his friends? Why didn't even one of them step forward on his behalf? Was he angry or hurt? What was he thinking as he plunged to the ground for the second time?

(*Pause for silent reflection.*)

Jesus, forgive us for the times we have failed to "be there" for our friends when they needed us. Help us to be as caring as you always are for us. Teach us how to follow you.

Eighth Station

The Women Weep for Jesus

Sometimes a crowd mentality takes over at school, on the bus, or at dances or parties. Things we would never do on our own seem okay when everyone else is doing them. We tend to cheer louder and crazier, dance harder and wilder, and even gang up more on "losers" when we're in a crowd.

The women in the crowd who wept for Jesus were crying because the situation called for tears. The crowd was stirred up and noisy. Frightening things were going on. The women were too curious to leave, but too afraid to keep quiet, and so they cried. As Jesus passed by he heard them. He told them to stop the phony crying, and to weep instead for the evil being done. He was asking them to follow their own hearts—not the crowd.

(Pause for silent reflection.)

Jesus, forgive us for the times we have gone along with the crowd without accepting responsibility for what we do. Help us to get in touch with what we really think and feel. Teach us how to follow you.

Ninth Station

Jesus Falls the Third Time

To be made fun of once is bad enough. To have it happen again and again is agony. Yet, there are people in our school, on our bus, in our neighborhood who are made fun of all the time. And we do it to them too. They don't fit in, they don't belong, so it's okay. Everyone does it, everyone knows how different they are. They "fall down" in front of us over and over, and we just knock them down again.

Jesus fell three times with the cross on his shoulders. All those people watching, what were they thinking? He had helped so many of them, but now not one of them had the courage to come forward. Were they frightened of the soldiers and the angry crowd? Or was it simply that Jesus was no longer one of them? And so they let him fall.

(Pause for silent reflection.)

Jesus, forgive us for the times we make fun of others. Give us the courage to lift them up when they fall, even if they don't "fit in." Teach us how to follow you.

Tenth Station

Jesus Is Stripped

Clothes are a big part of our lives. The right clothes cost a lot, sometimes more than we or our parents can afford, but we insist on having them. We want to look right; we have to be dressed like everyone else. There are people we know who don't dress right and we know what happens to them. Without the right clothes, they're nothing.

Jesus was stripped of his clothing in front of a whole crowd of people. He stood there without the comfort and security of his clothes. He was stripped of his dignity like a criminal. Without his clothes, how must he have felt?

(*Pause for silent reflection.*)

Jesus, forgive us for the times we have cared more for good clothes than for good people. Help us never to value "designer labels" more than the needs of others. Teach us how to follow you.

Eleventh Station

Jesus Is Nailed to the Cross

At times we do things that are ugly and wrong. We say hateful things about others: black people, white people, poor people, Hispanic people, Asian people. We call them names because they're different, and because we've decided that we're "better." We join others who laugh at them. Deep in our hearts we know this is wrong, but we go along with it anyway.

Jesus was the victim of anger and jealousy. He had stirred up the people. He had said and done "different" things. He had accepted all people equally—as they were. Now he was paying the price. There must have been those in the crowd who knew he was innocent, but they went along with the way things were. They stood by and let Jesus be nailed to the cross.

(Pause for silent reflection.)

Jesus, forgive us for the times we have nailed others to the cross because they were different. Show us how to love and value people as you did. Teach us how to follow you.

Twelfth Station

Jesus Dies on the Cross

We all think about dying from time to time. It's a thought that comes to us when things go wrong: when a boyfriend or girlfriend rejects us, or when our grades are slipping, or when we're drinking or smoking too much and can't seem to stop, or when parents are disappointed in everything we do. We are tempted to believe that death is easier than facing our problems.

Is this what Jesus was feeling as he died? Was he hoping to get it over with, or was he worried about his friends, his mother, his followers? Was he angry at God and at life? What did he mean when he said: "Forgive them; they don't know what they're doing"? Was he really so unselfish that he could pray for those who hurt him?

(Pause for silent reflection.)

Jesus, forgive us for the times we quit too easily because we're only thinking of ourselves. Share with us the kind of unselfish courage you had. Teach us how to follow you.

Thirteenth Station

Jesus Is Taken Down from the Cross

Sometimes we clearly recognize a lost cause: a school team that never wins, a band that can't make good music, a friendship completely broken. We don't want to be part of a lost cause. But often we are. We're on that losing team, or in that band, or part of that broken relationship. What then?

Joseph of Arimathea, a secret follower of Jesus who was afraid of the leaders, finally came forward after Jesus had died. He claimed the body of this "criminal." What made him do it? Wasn't he still afraid of being identified with a lost cause? No doubt he was ashamed for waiting so long, but at least he did something good and courageous in the end.

(Pause for silent reflection.)

Jesus, forgive us for the times we walk away from painful situations and from the people in them. Give us the courage to act on our beliefs, no matter how afraid we feel. Teach us how to follow you.

Fourteenth Station

Jesus Is Placed in the Tomb

When we have worked hard at something, we expect to be rewarded: a good grade, praise from our parents, cheers from the fans. We certainly don't want to be blamed or punished for doing our best. It happens sometimes though to people we know, and we walk away from them. We don't want to hang out with losers.

Jesus spent his public life preaching, healing, and helping others. He promised good things to those who followed him. But here he was, dead from crucifixion, and apparently good things had not happened to him or to those who believed in him. At this moment of sorrow and failure, his followers had abandoned him, and he was buried in another man's grave.

(*Pause for silent reflection.*)

Jesus, forgive us for the times we have measured our success by the applause and praise of others. Help us learn to look beneath the surface of things with the eyes of faith. Teach us how to follow you.

An Easter Prayer

Jesus, we know that your story didn't end on Good Friday. Your "failure" was turned into victory on Easter morning. "Jesus is not here," your messenger said: "he has been raised from the dead."

As your followers, we know that rejection, loss, even death and dying, don't necessarily mean failure. With your help, we can move through these experiences toward new life and resurrection. We can be turned around—as you were. Give us the courage, please, to accept the reality that life will always have its bright sides and its dark sides, its joys and sorrows. And help us to believe that God has good things in store for us, too.

Amen. Alleluia.